WHY DO I CRY?

BY Emilie Dufresne

All rights reserved.
Printed in Malaysia.

A catalogue record for this book is available from the British Library.

ISBN: 978-1-78998-053-0

Written by:
Emilie Dufresne

Edited by:
John Wood

Designed by:
Danielle Rippengill

©2019
The Secret Book Company
King's Lynn
Norfolk PE30 4LS

All facts, statistics, web addresses and URLs in this book were verified as valid and accurate at time of writing. No responsibility for any changes to external websites or references can be accepted by either the author or publisher.

IMAGE CREDITS

All images are courtesy of Shutterstock.com, unless otherwise specified. With thanks to Getty Images, Thinkstock Photo and iStockphoto. Front Cover & 1 – Dmitry Natashin, Nadzin, newelle, Rvector. Images used on every spread – Nadzin, TheFarAwayKingdom. 2 – johavel. 4&5 – Iconic Bestiary. 6 – johavel. 7 – Rvector. 8 – Jane Kelly. 9&10 – Iconic Bestiary. 11 – svtdesign. 12&13 – LOVE YOU. 14 – Iconic Bestiary. 15 – Alena Ohneva. 16 – Iconic Bestiary. 17 – Sim Lev, Alena Ohneva. 18 – Rvector, Ienjoyeverytime. 19 – Ienjoyeverytime. 20 – newelle, Rvector, GraphicsRF. 21 – Nadia Buravleva, hvostik. 22& 23 – Iconic Bestiary. 23 – newelle, Rvector.

CONTENTS

PAGE 4	**Are Your Eyes Watering?**
PAGE 6	**Types of Tear**
PAGE 10	**Making Tears**
PAGE 12	**Journey of a Tear**
PAGE 14	**What's in a Tear?**
PAGE 16	**Feeling Better?**
PAGE 18	**Eye Bogies**
PAGE 20	**Gloopy Eyes**
PAGE 22	**Cry Babies**
PAGE 23	**Activity**
PAGE 24	**Glossary and Index**

Words that look like **this** can be found in the glossary on page 24.

ARE YOUR EYES WATERING?

It doesn't matter how big and brave you are; if you've ever felt sad or hurt yourself, you've probably wanted to cry.

Everybody cries, especially when they stub their toe on the corner of the sofa.

We all cry for lots of different reasons. It might be because we are very sad, very happy, or because our bodies are hurting.

Crying is a perfectly normal thing to do. But why do we do it?

TYPES OF TEAR

Not all tears are the same. We actually make three different types of tear:

Everyone is different, and this means we cry at different things.

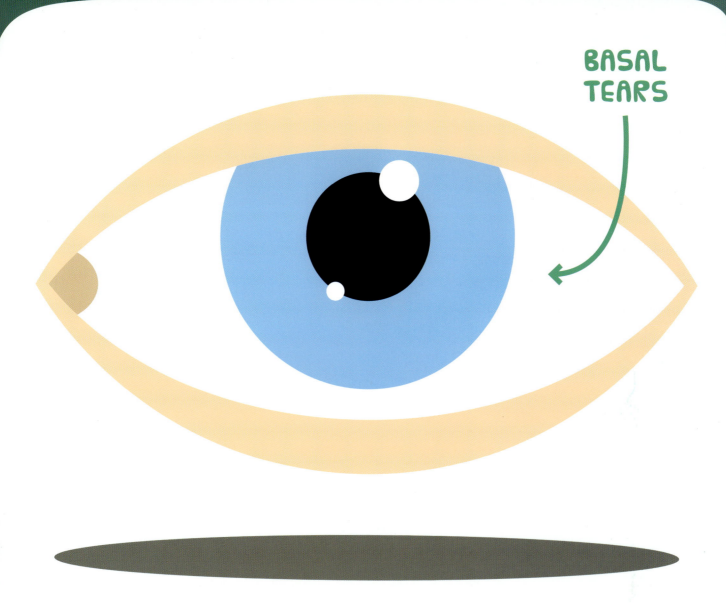

BASAL TEARS

Basal Tears

We always have basal tears in our eyes. They **lubricate** our eyes so that they don't get too dry. These tears are spread around the eye by blinking.

Reflex Tears

Our bodies produce reflex tears when something **irritates** our eyes. This could be things such as **allergens** or smoke.

The fumes from cutting onions can create reflex tears too.

Emotional Tears

We cry emotional tears when we have strong feelings or are in pain. If we hurt ourselves or have a shock, this can make us cry emotional tears too.

We even cry emotional tears when we are very happy.

MAKING TEARS

The lacrimal **(SAY: LAK-RI-MUL) system** is made up of organs and body parts that allow us to make and drain away tears. The most important parts are the eyes and nose.

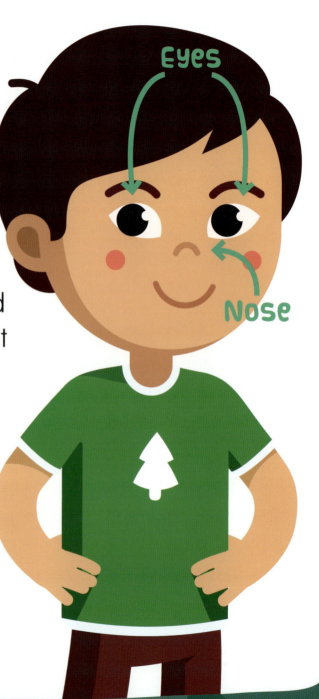

Organs are parts of our bodies that do certain jobs.

When we need to cry, for any reason, our brain sends a message to our body to start up our lacrimal system and we begin to cry.

JOURNEY OF A TEAR

STEP 1: The tears come out of the **LACRIMAL GLANDS** behind the top of the eye.

STEP 2: Some tears are drained away from our eyes through the **TEAR DUCTS** at the corner of our eyes.

STEP 3: These are then taken to the **LACRIMAL SAC**.

STEP 5:
If our ducts can't drain our tears away quick enough, the tears run down our face.

STEP 4:
The tears are then drained away through the nose – that's why your nose gets runny when you cry!

When we cry, it puts a lot of stress on the muscles in our face and can give us a bad headache.

WHAT'S IN A TEAR?

All tears have three basic layers.

Layer one:
This oily layer stops tears from evaporating (SAY: EE-VAP-OR-ATE-ING).

Layer two:
This layer holds water and minerals, such as salt - that's why your tears taste salty!

Layer three:
A layer of mucus that helps to keep the tear on the eye.

When we cry because of emotion or pain, other things are released by our glands. Lots of hormones build up in our bodies when we feel emotional, or experience pain.

Crying releases some of these hormones.

FEELING BETTER?

Have you ever heard people say that they have "had a good cry"? But how can crying make us feel better?

Well, it's all about those hormones!

As we cry, all the stress hormones our body has built up are washed away with our tears, taking the stress out of our body.

Tears can also help us feel less pain!

EYE BOGIES

Sometimes we wake up with eye bogies in the corner of our eyes. These can be dry and crusty, or wet and stringy. Both are normal!

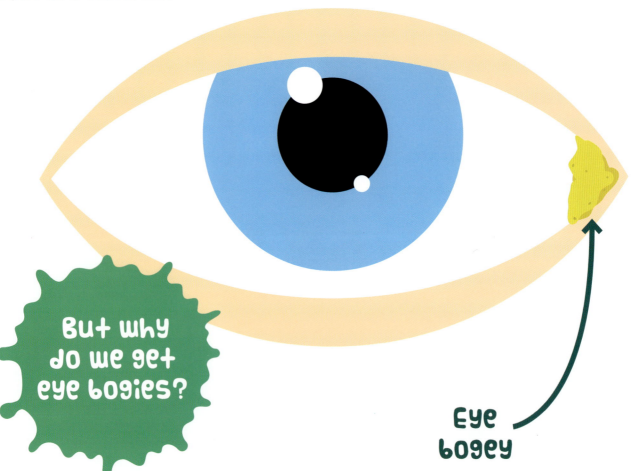

But why do we get eye bogies?

Eye bogey

Not all of the oil from our basal tears is washed away. Eye bogies are a mixture of this oil and any dust in our eyes.

These gather at the corner of our eyes and dry, turning crusty.

GLOOPY EYES

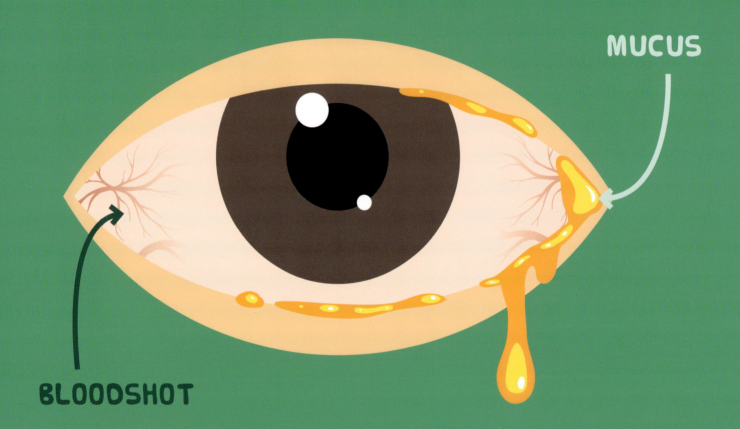

MUCUS

BLOODSHOT

Sometimes our eyes can get **infected**. They may become bloodshot, itchy, or a bit sticky from mucus. One type of eye infection is called conjunctivitis **(SAY: CON-JUNK-TIV-EYE-TUS)**.

To help prevent eye infections, make sure you:

WASH YOUR HANDS REGULARLY

DON'T RUB YOUR EYES TOO MUCH

CRY BABIES

Babies can't talk, so they use their tears to tell us when they need something. Most of these tears aren't because the baby is in pain, but because they need our attention.

Babies cry when they are hungry, tired, unwell or when their nappies are wet.

ACTIVITY

Can you work out if these tears are reflex or emotional?

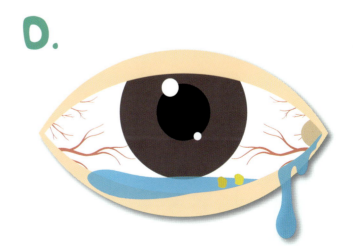

Answers: A. Emotional; B. Emotional; C. Emotional; D. Reflex

GLOSSARY

allergens — things that cause an allergic reaction

evaporating — turning from a liquid into a gas or vapour, usually through heat

infected — when germs or disease have entered part of the body

irritates — when something aggravates part of the body, making it red, sore or itchy

lubricate — to cover something in something slippery

minerals — important things that plants, animals or humans need to grow

mucus — a slimy substance that helps to protect and lubricate certain parts of the human body

system — a set of things that work together to do specific jobs

INDEX

body 5, 8, 10–11, 15, 17
glands 12, 15
happiness 5, 9
hormones 15–17
noses 10, 13
oils 14, 19
pain 9, 15, 17, 22
sadness 4–5
stress 13, 17
tears:
- **basal** 6–7, 19
- **emotional** 6, 9, 15, 23
- **reflex** 6, 8, 23